VOLUME 4

Earth Science

By

Jason Georges and Tracy Irons-Georges

Editorial Consultants
Karen E. Kalumuck, Ph.D.
Charles W. Rogers, Ph.D.
Elizabeth D. Schafer, Ph.D.

ROURKE CORPORATION, INC.
VERO BEACH, FLORIDA 32964

Printed in the United States of America.

Library of Congress Cataloging-in-Publication Data

Georges, Jason, 1969-
    Rourke's world of science encyclopedia/Jason Georges and Tracy Irons-Georges.
        p.   cm.
    Includes bibliographical references and index.
    Contents: Human life — Animal life — Plant life — Earth science — Chemistry — Physics — Astronomy & Space — Mathematics — Technology.
    ISBN 0-86593-482-7
    1. Science — Encyclopedias, Juvenile, 2. Technology-Encyclopedias, Juvenile. [1. Science—Encyclopedias.] I. Irons -Georges, Tracy.   II. Title.
Q121.G44 1998
503—dc21   98-6605
                                               CIP
                                             AC

Photographs: © PhotoDisc, pages 4, 6-7, 10, 12, 13, 14, 15, 17, 18-19, 21, 25, 26, 27, 28, 29, 30, 31, 32, 35, 40, 41, 42, 44, 45, 46, 48, 50, 51, 53, 54, 58; page 22, © Peter Menzel/PNI; Page 23, © Steve McCutcheon, 1964/PNI; page 24, © Marcelo Brodsky/L. Stock/West Light; page 34, © Carl Zeiss, 1988/PNI; pages 36-39, © Weatherstock; page 47, © Carl Purcell, 1995/PNI; page 49, © Phil Schofield, 1988/PNI; page 55, © J.B. Diederich, 1988/PNI; page 60, © Chuck Nacke, 1987/PNI; page 61, © Yoav Levy, 1994/PNI.

Illustration: page 9, Paul Calderon.

Table of Contents

■ What Is Earth Science?

The **Earth** is our planet. It is home to all the plants, animals, and humans that we know about. The air, water, and land of the planet make it possible for life to exist. Everything on the planet needs everything else.

The Earth is the third planet from the Sun. It revolves around, or **orbits**, the Sun once every year. The Earth spins, or **rotates**, as it orbits the Sun. It rotates once every 24 hours. The Sun seems to rise in the east and set in the west. The imaginary line around the middle of the Earth is called the **equator** (ih-KWAY-tur). The half of the Earth above the equator is called the **Northern Hemisphere** (HEH-muh-sfeer). The half of

the Earth below the equator is called the Southern Hemisphere. At the top and bottom of the planet are the poles.

Earth science is the study of the planet Earth and how it works.

● The Origin of Our Planet

The Earth was created over 4 billion years ago. It came from a cloud of dust and gas particles swirling in space. Some of the dust and gas formed into the Sun. The rest of the particles swirled around each other until they became round. They formed the planets in the Solar System.

The young Earth looked very different than it does today. Intense heat inside the growing planet caused molten, or liquid, rock to form. The hot surface slowly cooled over millions of years. Water vapor and other gases made the air, or atmosphere (AT-moh-sfeer). Clouds covered the planet. Rain helped cool the hot surface. Cooling rocks slowly began to soak up the falling rain. Oceans formed when the ground could hold no more water.

Land above the level of the ocean formed large pieces of land called continents (KON-tun-untz). Eventually, the clouds became thinner and sunlight could shine through. The Earth still looked very different than it does today. Heat and other forces from inside the planet continued changing the surface. Over billions of years, the Earth evolved into the way it is today.

● The Earth Today

From outer space, the Earth looks very blue because most of the planet is covered with water. Nearly 3/4 of the Earth is oceans, seas, lakes, rivers, and other bodies of water. The rest of the planet is covered by five continents. Huge sheets of ice are at the poles.

The ocean is the source of most of the water on the planet. It provides much of the water that makes clouds in the sky. Water rises up into the air when it **evaporates** (uh-VAH-pore-ates). This means that it turns into a mist you cannot see. The water comes back down to the ground as rain. Rain fills the lakes, rivers, and streams on the land. Plants and animals need this water to survive.

The Earth is a living planet with different **environments** (in-VI-run-muntz). These are the places on the planet where life exists. The ocean has various environments within it.

Deserts, prairies, forests, and mountains are all types of environments on the land. Every environment depends on a balance between its soil, air, water, plants, and animals.

The Parts of the Earth

Much of the surface of our planet is underwater, mostly under the oceans. The rest of the surface is called **land**. Below the surface are different layers of rocks and other materials. Above the surface are different layers of air. All of these parts work together to make life on Earth possible.

Most of the Earth's surface is covered in water.

● Earth's Layers

There are three major layers from the surface of the planet to its center. They are the crust, the mantle, and the core. The top, thinnest layer of the Earth is called the **crust**. The crust is thicker in different parts. It is about 5 miles thick under the oceans. It can be over 40 miles thick below the tallest mountains. All life on the planet lives above the crust.

Below the crust is the **mantle**. The mantle is a very thick layer. It goes down over 1,800 miles (2,900 kilometers). Most rocks of the Earth are in the mantle. Rocks in the mantle are more **dense**. This means that they are packed a lot closer than rocks in the crust. They are under the weight of all the rocks on top of them. The tempera-

SECTION OF THE EARTH'S CRUST

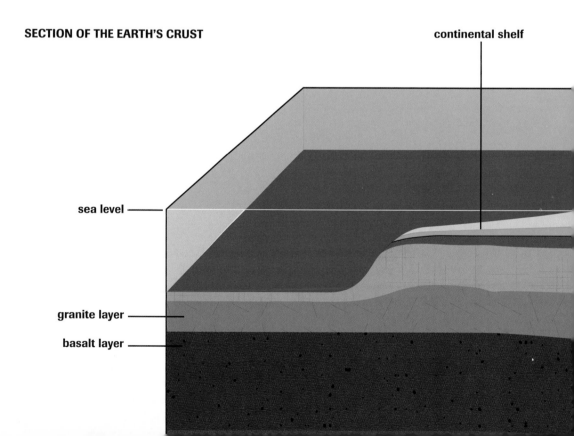

continental shelf

sea level

granite layer

basalt layer

ture in the mantle is very hot. Some rocks even melt.

The middle of the Earth is called the **core**. The core has two different layers of its own. Directly beneath the mantle is the **outer core**. The outer core goes over 1,000 miles (2,000 kilometers) below the mantle. It is made up of a combination of the metals iron and nickel. There may even be sulfur in the outer core. The outer core is a liquid because it is so hot and under so much pressure. At the center of the Earth is the **inner core**. The inner core is made of solid metal. From the edge of the inner core to the center of the earth is about 850 miles (1,370 kilometers). It also is made of iron and nickel and is very hot. It is solid metal because the pressure is so high.

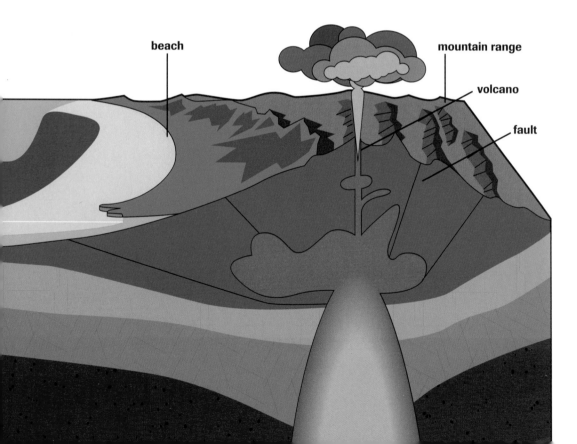

● Rocks

The crust of the Earth has three basic kinds of rock. They are **igneous** (IG-nee-us), **metamorphic** (meh-tuh-MORE-fick), and **sedimentary** (seh-duh-MEN-tuh-ree) rocks. The substances that make up most of rocks are called **minerals** (MIH-nuh-rulz). The most common type of rocks in the crust are igneous rocks. They are formed with the cooling of **magma** (MAG-muh),

hot liquid rock from the crust and mantle. These rocks include **granite** (GRAH-nut) above the oceans and **basalt** (BUH-salt) below the ocean floor. Metamorphic rocks are made when one type of rock changes into another because of high temperatures or pressures. Diamonds are made when carbon is put under a lot of pressure and heat. Sedimentary rocks are made from parts of other rocks, chemicals, or the remains of dead plants and animals.

Sedimentary rocks often form layers in the crust. These layers are called **strata** (STRA-tuh). Each layer tells about Earth's past. Strata near the surface are newer than those further underground. Old bones, or

fossils, from plants and animals are sometimes found in different strata. The history of the Earth learned from these fossils is called the **fossil record**.

Scientists have used the fossil record to create a history of the Earth since life first evolved. This is called the **geologic time scale**. Simple living things first appeared almost 4 billion years ago during the **Precambrian** (pre-KAME-bree-un) **era**. The earliest fish, reptiles, and land plants evolved during the **Paleozoic** (pay-lee-uh-ZOH-ick) **era**. The dinosaurs were alive during the next period, called the **Mesozoic** (meh-zuh-ZOH-ick) **era**. They suddenly became extinct 65 million years ago. Large mammals and humans evolved in the most recent period, the **Cenozoic** (seh-nuh-ZOH-ick) **era**.

GETTING TO KNOW...

Andrija Mohorovicic

Andrija Mohorovicic (mah-har-ah-VEE-cheech) was born in 1857 in what is now Croatia (kroh-AY-shuh). He earned a degree in mathematics and physics. Mohorovicic studied the atmosphere and set up a weather station.

In 1901, a strong earthquake was felt in Croatia. Mohorovicic became interested in **seismology** (size-MAW-luh-jee), the study of earthquakes. He got a **seismograph** (SIZE-muh-graf), a device that measures earthquakes. A very destructive earthquake happened in Croatia in 1909. Mohorovicic studied the seismograph recordings. Waves of energy from the earthquakes were reflected by a change in density under the Earth's surface. This **discontinuity** (dis-kon-tuh-NEW-uh-tee) is the line between the crust and the mantle. It occurs all over the world. The layer is now called the **Moho** (MOH-hoh), after Mohorovicic.

● The Ocean

The ocean is very important to life on our planet. The first living things evolved in the ocean. Today, many plants and animals live in the sea. Much of the weather on Earth is controlled by this large body of water. How the ocean moves also has a big effect on life on land.

Tides are the rising and falling of the ocean level near the shore. A high tide is when the water level rises.

A low tide is when the water level falls. This movement is mostly controlled by the Moon. The gravity of the Moon pulls the water in the ocean toward it. The Sun also affects the tides. It is larger than the Moon and has more gravity, but the Sun does not pull on the oceans as strongly as the Moon. The Sun is much farther away from the Earth. Plants and animals near the shore spend their lives adapting to high and low tides. Land at the shores, called coastlines, is built up and torn down by the movement of the ocean tides.

The coastlines are also changed by the movement of waves. Beaches are made by waves, which break up rocks into smooth pieces of sand. Waves can form in several ways. Tides are actually the largest waves. Most smaller waves on the surface of the ocean or a lake are caused by the wind. Waves formed by strong winds in the middle of the ocean can make waves that hit a beach very far away. Waves can also be formed by underwater earthquakes or eruptions of volcanoes. A giant wave called a **tsunami** (soo-NAW-mee) can be made in this way. It is sometimes called a **tidal wave**, even though it is not like tides. A tsunami causes great destruction if it reaches land.

● The Atmosphere

An atmosphere is the layer of gases that covers the surface of a planet. Most planets have some kind of atmosphere. The atmosphere of Earth lets many different organisms live on the land and in the water. It is very important to all plants and animals. The atmosphere protects our planet from dangerous radiation from the Sun. It also provides gases that animals need to

breathe and that plants need to make food. Earth's atmosphere is made mostly of **nitrogen** (NI-truh-jun) and **oxygen** (AWK-sih-jun), with small amounts of argon, carbon dioxide, hydrogen, methane, and other gases. Ash from volcanoes, dust, and small drops of water called **vapor** are also in the atmosphere.

Earth's atmosphere has many different layers. The one closest to the surface is called the **troposphere** (TROH-puh-sfeer). It is where most changes in the weather happen. The layer above the troposphere is the **stratosphere** (STRAH-troh-sfeer). The stratosphere contains the ozone layer. **Ozone** (OH-zone) is a form of oxygen that stops most of the Sun's ultraviolet radiation from reaching the lower part of the atmosphere. The **mesosphere** (MEH-zuh-sfeer) is the next layer up, followed by the **thermosphere** (THUR-muh-sfeer). The **ionosphere** (i-AH-nuh-sfeer) is the highest layer in the atmosphere. It reflects radio waves and its height is affected by the Sun. The changing height of the ionosphere increases the range of radio stations after dark.

■ Forces That Shape the Earth

Many forces can form, or shape, the Earth. Some of these forces come from deep within the ground. Volcanoes and earthquakes cause major changes to the landscape. Other changes occur as a result of natural forces on the surface. Water and wind shape the planet every day. Human activity is also playing a role in shaping the world.

● Plate Tectonics

A long time ago, the Earth looked very different than it looks today. The surface of the Earth is made of huge pieces of crust called **plates**. The plates make up all land and the ocean floor. Plates come together to form **ridges** on land and underwater. They form **trenches** where they separate from one another. A plate grows bigger on one edge where new igneous rock is formed. The other edge of the plate slides under or on top of another plate. This growth and movement of plates is called **plate tectonics** (tek-TAW-nicks). Plate tectonics causes earthquakes to shake, volcanoes to erupt, mountains to grow, and continents to move.

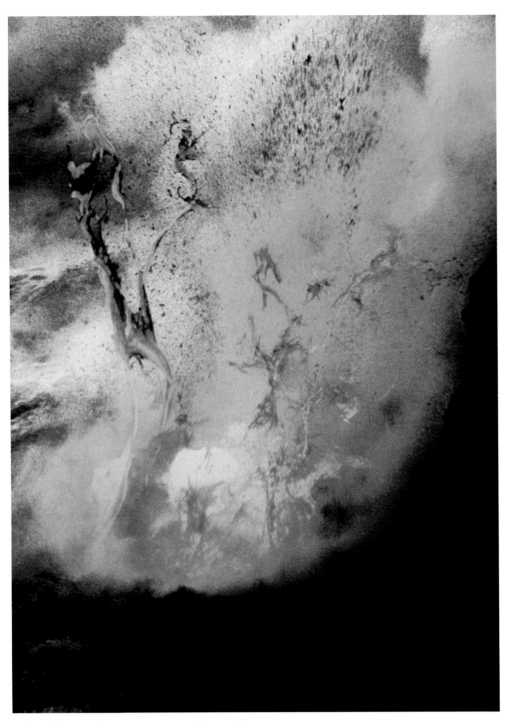

Volcanic eruptions can occur where plates meet.

● Continental Drift

Africa, Europe, North America, South America, Asia, Australia, and India were all connected once. This supercontinent was called **Pangaea** (pan-JEE-uh), which means "all lands." Pangaea broke up about 200 million years ago. Its pieces drifted apart over time into the continents as we know them today. The process of the continents moving is called **continental drift**.

GETTING TO KNOW...

Alfred Wegener

Alfred Wegener (VAY-geh-nair) was born in Germany in 1880. He dreamed of exploring Greenland and the Arctic. In school, Wegener studied astronomy, meteorology, and geophysics (gee-oh-FIH-zicks), the study of the forces that shape the Earth. He fought in World War I and was wounded twice.

Wegener is best known for his ideas about continental drift. He looked at a map of the world. He noticed the similar shapes of the coasts of Africa and South America. Wegener suggested that they were once joined and then drifted apart. He published his theories in the book *The Origin of Continents and Oceans* in 1924. Wegener died in 1930. It was not until the 1960's that discoveries confirmed that continental drift really happens.

Plate tectonics cause the continents to drift. Deep in the oceans are giant trenches called **rift valleys**. The plates on which the continents sit spread away from these valleys. The plates move apart as new material from within the Earth comes up. In some places, an ocean plate will slide below a continental plate. Mountains are often pushed up along the plate that stays on top. The Andes (AN-deez) in South America formed this way. Sometimes, two continental plates collide. This causes the plates to crumple and high mountains to form. India collided with Asia and made the Himalayas (hih-muh-LAY-uhz).

● Volcanoes

A volcano (vawl-KAY-noh) is a hole where hot rock and gas comes out, or **erupts**. Magma deep within the Earth puts pressure on weak areas of the crust. The magma melts away rock and creates hot gases. The gas and magma come together many miles or kilometers underground in the magma chamber. Pressure builds. A volcano will erupt when the pressure becomes high enough.

When a volcano erupts, it blasts a hole or vent to the surface. Magma that reaches the surface is called **lava** (LAH-vuh). An eruption sends out lava, hot gases, and ash. Volcanoes erupt in many ways. Some volcanoes send out towers of lava and clouds of ash. Other volcanoes ooze rivers of lava. Many volcanoes explode violently.

Volcanoes usually occur on or near the edges of the plates in the crust. They often erupt when the plates move. Volcanoes in the ocean can create islands. The islands of Hawaii were formed this way.

DID YOU KNOW…

A Mountain Can Explode

In May of 1980, the volcano Mount St. Helens erupted in Washington State. It had been dormant for over 120 years. The north side of the mountain collapsed, and the top exploded. The blast sent ash high into the atmosphere and flattened trees!

Volcanoes on land sometimes make mountains. Active volcanoes still erupt sometimes. **Dormant volcanoes** have not erupted in a long time but might. **Extinct volcanoes** will never erupt again.

Volcanoes in the ocean can create islands.

● Earthquakes

An **earthquake** is a sudden movement of the crust. It is caused by a quick release of energy within the ground. Most earthquakes occur along the edges of the plates. The places where they origi- nate are called **faults**. Faults are usually cracks along the edges of the plates. Some are in the middle of the plates. Most faults run deep into the crust.

The rocks on both sides of the fault fit tightly together. The rocks bend as stress builds up because of continental drift. If the stress gets strong enough, the rocks suddenly snap back into shape and release shock waves of energy. The point where the stress is released is called the focus of an earthquake. The

The San Andreas fault runs through California.

place on the Earth's surface directly above the focus is called the **epicenter** (EH-puh-sen-tur). The shock waves reach the surface of the Earth. The land starts to shake.

There are several ways to measure earthquakes. The **Richter** (RICK-tur) **scale** describes the strength, or **magnitude** (MAG-nuh-tood), of an earthquake. It is named after American scientist Charles Richter. Earthquakes with Richter magnitudes greater than 6.0 can cause a lot of damage. The **Mercalli** (mair-KAW-lee) **scale** measures how much the Earth shakes. It is named after Italian scientist Giuseppe Mercalli. Earthquakes with a Mercalli intensity of I (one) are barely felt. Those with an intensity of XII (twelve) cause total destruction. Scientists also study earthquake waves to learn about the interior of the Earth.

● Glaciers

Glaciers (GLAY-shurs) are big sheets of ice. The ice from glaciers usually does not melt from year to year. Glaciers form when layer upon layer of snow is compressed into ice. They begin to move as the ice builds up and becomes denser. Glaciers slowly move down hills and valleys like a river of ice. They can carry huge rocks with them. They often carve deep valleys as they move. Glaciers make mountain peaks and ridges more sharp. They also make valley walls more steep. Three glaciers around a mountain in Switzerland created a peak called the Matterhorn.

Some glaciers are in South America. This one is in Tierra del Fuego, Argentina.

The Arctic Circle has many glaciers.

Today, many glaciers are small. They can be found in mountain valleys where it stays cold and shady. The largest glaciers are in Antarctica and Greenland. These huge masses of ice are called continental glaciers. They are so big that they cool the air and water far away from the glacier.

Glaciers covered more of the Earth at various times in the past called **ice ages**. The temperature of the planet became a lot colder during ice ages. Huge continental glaciers covered much of North America and Europe. Water levels in the oceans dropped over 300 feet (about 100 meters) as the glaciers grew. The landscape was changed when the glaciers eventually melted.

● Erosion

Everything on the surface of the Earth changes. Forces like sunlight, wind, rain, and snow all influence the way the environment changes and decays, or breaks down over time. This decay is called **erosion** (ih-ROH-zhun). Weather causes the most erosion. Wind, rain, and frost make many rocks fall apart. Other forms of erosion affect the chemical structure of things. This is called chemical weathering.

Water in all forms causes erosion. Erosion from ocean waves can take away sand from beaches, create bays, hollow out caves, and change shorelines. Rain often washes away loose topsoil. Rain can sometimes make hillsides very wet and cause landslides. Over time, rivers sometimes wear away rocks and form valleys and **canyons**. The Grand Canyon was formed over millions of years. Many layers of sedimentary rock can be seen in the sides of the canyon wall.

The Grand Canyon has been formed by erosion over millions of years.

Wind can also change landscapes dramatically. Particles of sand and dust grind down the surfaces of rocks and objects they are blown  across. Strong winds can change the shape of piles of sand, called **dunes**, in deserts and on beaches.

FIND OUT MORE ABOUT...

Caves

Sometimes, erosion takes place underground. Caves are formed when water wears away rocks. Rainwater contains an acid that dissolves limestone. Caves often form because of streams that flow underground. The stream flows just above the **water table**. The water table is the level at which the ground is made completely wet, or saturated (SAH-chuh-ray-tud), by water. Underground rivers sometimes form a series of branching caves. An empty cave, or **cavern**, is left when the water table goes down.

Sometimes, water drips, or seeps, into caves through the rocks above. This water can pick up minerals. Minerals left behind in the cave are called deposits. Deposits form on the roof of a cave when water drips. They make **stalactites** (stuh-LAK-tite) that hang down from the top of a cave. More deposits are formed as the water drips to the floor of the cave. Eventually, deposits on the floor will form a **stalagmite** (stuh-LAG-mite) that comes up from the floor of the cave. A **column** is formed when a stalactite and a stalagmite meet.

● Human Activities

Natural forces have shaped the Earth since its origin. Only recently have people had an effect on the Earth. Humans can change the surface of the Earth in many ways. Mountains can be flattened, and valleys can be filled in. Sometimes, people dig caves in mountains called **mines** to bring out minerals. **Tunnels** through mountains are used for transportation. People may carve mountains into monuments, like Mount Rushmore in South Dakota.

Under the sea, coral reefs are formed in the wrecks of sunken ships. They provide a new place for sea creatures to live. **Harbors** and walls called **breakwaters** are constructed by moving piles of dirt and rocks into the ocean. They prevent waves from destroying ships.

Mount Rushmore, South Dakota.

People can dig a **canal** to link two bodies of water. The Panama Canal connects the Atlantic Ocean and the Pacific Ocean. People can move rivers to provide water to areas that do not have enough. These rivers sometimes flow through **aqueducts** (AH-kwuh-ductz). Sometimes, lakes are made by building a dam across a river. **Dams** provide energy to communities. **Hydroelectric** (hi-droh-uh-LECK-trick) energy is electricity made using the power of water.

■ Weather

Many things on Earth depend on the weather. Air and water can be hot, cold, or somewhere in between. Air can have a lot of water, or moisture, in it or none at all. Plants and animals need some water to survive, and many can live only in certain temperatures. The general type of weather conditions for a place is called the climate. Sometimes, weather causes problems. It can even be dangerous.

Strong winds create hurricanes.

● **Wind**

Moving air is called **wind**. This movement is created by changes in pressure in the atmosphere. Pressure is affected by temperatures. Low pressure occurs in areas with warm air, and high pressure occurs in areas with cold air. Some winds happen only in smaller areas like cities, towns, canyons, and valleys. These winds are low to the ground. A light wind is called a **breeze**. It may move leaves and flags. A sudden stronger wind is called a **gust**. Strong winds can knock over trees and power lines. Winds that blow across deserts are usually warm. Winds that blow across mountains are often cold, especially when there is snow. The **windchill factor** is how much colder it feels outside when a cold wind is blowing. Some winds occur across very large areas like continents and oceans. These winds are higher up in the atmosphere. They move clouds. Fast winds high in the sky are called **jet streams**.

PROJECTS
Volume 10
Page 17

A windmill can be used to make energy.

● Clouds

Clouds are formed when moisture on the Earth's surface evaporates. It rises into the atmosphere where it is too cold to stay as mist. The water molecules stick to particles like dust to make drops of water or crystals of ice. Many drops of water form a cloud. The cloud either evaporates or falls back down as mist, rain, hail, snow, or sleet. The falling of moisture to the

Earth is called **precipitation** (prih-sih-puh-TAY-shun).

Clouds come in many shapes and sizes. **Cumulus** (KYOO-myuh-lus) clouds are tall and puffy like cotton. They can start near the ground and extend far up into the sky. **Cirrus** (SIR-us) clouds are thin and wispy. They are high in the atmosphere. **Stratus** (STRAH-tus) clouds form a large layer or sheet in the sky. A **thundercloud** gives off electricity in the form of **lightning**. A flash of lightning makes the surrounding air expand, which causes a loud sound called **thunder**. A thundercloud does not always bring rain. **Fog** is a large cloud of mist that forms very low to the ground. It can be thick and hard to see through.

● Rain

Water that falls from the sky is called **rain**. Rain can have very small drops of water that is almost like mist. It can have larger drops but not very many of them. This is sometimes called sprinkles or drizzle. **Showers** are short periods of rain that can be heavier. A **downpour** is a heavy, often sudden rain. A **rainstorm** has heavy rains and often strong winds. A **thunderstorm** also has lightning and thunder.

Heavy rains can cause damage to houses and nature and can hurt people. This is especially true if it rains a lot very quickly or constantly over a long time. A **flood** happens when water rises in rivers or lakes and flows over areas that are usually dry. The water in a flood can rise slowly or can move very fast like a river. A **flash flood** is a flood that happens quickly when a lot of rain falls in a small area. There is little time for warnings. Floods can cover houses, wash away roads and bridges, and drown people. Sometimes, a hillside gets too much rain and cannot soak up any more water. The top layer of soil falls down. This is called a **mudslide**.

DID YOU KNOW...

You Can Tell the Distance to a Thunderstorm

We see lightning when it occurs, but the sound of thunder takes several seconds to reach us. When you are near a thunderstorm, watch for a flash of lightning and count until you hear thunder. Every five seconds is a mile, and every three seconds is a kilometer!

● Snow

Rain often starts out as ice crystals high in the atmosphere. The crystals melt into raindrops if the air on the way down is above freezing. The crystals stay as snow if the air on the way down is below freezing. **Snow** is falling water in the form of ice flakes. Every **snowflake** is a little different than the rest. They all have six sides, but some also have needles, stars, or other shapes.

Larger snowflakes form when the temperature is near freezing. The snowflakes are wet and stick together as they fall through the sky. Smaller snowflakes form when the air is colder.

Sleet is made of frozen raindrops that bounce when they hit the ground. **Hail** is made of larger frozen raindrops. They can fall during thunderstorms. Most pieces of hail are small, but some can be the size of a golf ball or bigger. Large hail can damage crops and even hurt people.

Snowflake

A lot of snow may fall in an area. Snow can block roads and doors. Being snowed in means you cannot get outside because there is so much snow on the ground. Sometimes, deep snow on the side of a mountain will suddenly slide down. This is called an **avalanche** (A-vuh-lanch). An avalanche can bury people, often skiers or hikers.

● **Tornadoes**

PROJECTS
Volume 10
Page 18

A tornado (tore-NAY-doh) is a small, violent storm with winds that spin very fast. It is also called a **cyclone** (SI-klone) or a whirlwind. A tornado usually forms inside thunderclouds. Areas of cold air pull in warm, moist air to make an area of low pressure. A cloud turns around the low pressure until it makes a spinning cone called a **funnel**. The funnel usually stays in the air, but it can hit the ground, or touch down, suddenly.

The funnel of a tornado twists in the air before it touches down.

Small tornadoes may break tree branches and street signs. Larger ones can break windows, pull out trees, flip over cars, and knock down walls. The biggest tornadoes can destroy houses

and other buildings, killing many people. Many tornadoes occur in the United States from Texas to Nebraska in what is called Tornado Alley. Texas, Florida, and Oklahoma have the most tornadoes each year. Cold air from the north and warm air from the Gulf of Mexico meet in these places.

GETTING TO KNOW...

Vilhelm Bjerknes

Vilhelm Bjerknes (BYERK-nays) was born in Norway in 1862. He worked with his father, a physicist who studied the motion of fluids. This is called **hydrodynamics** (hi-droh-di-NAH-micks). Bjerknes heard about the research of Heinrich Hertz on electrical waves. He became Hertz's assistant.

Bjerknes earned a Ph.D. and returned to hydrodynamics. He used this work to study the atmosphere and the oceans. His ideas helped start **meteorology** (mee-tee-RAW-luh-jee), the science of the atmosphere and weather. Bjerknes and his son set up weather stations to collect information. Their results suggested the polar front theory to explain how a cyclone forms. A **front** is the area between different masses of air. Bjerknes said that cyclones happen where warm and cold fronts meet.

● Hurricanes

A hurricane (HER-uh-kane) is a cyclone that forms in tropical regions, places near the equator. A hurricane starts as a **tropical storm** with strong winds. It spins around an area of low pressure. A tropical storm is called a hurricane when the winds reach high speeds of about 74 miles (119 kilometers) per hour. A hurricane always forms over water. It usually lasts from five to seven days and slows down when it reaches land. A hurricane often brings rain and lightning in addition to its strong winds.

A hurricane can cause a lot of destruction on islands and along coastlines.

The center of the hurricane is the **eye**. Clouds spin around the eye and carry a lot of moisture. It is strangely calm inside the eye of a hurricane. There may be sunshine, warmer air, and

almost no wind. Some people in the eye of a hurricane think that the storm is over, but the second part will come in a few minutes or hours. Strong hurricanes can destroy buildings and boats and can kill many people. The worst hurricanes often form in the Atlantic Ocean. They cause a lot of damage on Caribbean islands and in the southern and eastern United States.

FIND OUT MORE ABOUT...

The Seasons

The Earth is tilted in one direction as it orbits the Sun. It leans like a spinning top as it moves through space. Half of the Earth is tilted toward the Sun. The Northern Hemisphere gets more sunlight when the Earth is on one side of the Sun. There, summer has long days and hot temperatures. Not as much sunlight reaches the Southern Hemisphere. There, summer has shorter days and colder temperatures. Half a year later, the Southern Hemisphere receives more sunlight and has warm weather. At this time, it is winter in the Northern Hemisphere.

The equator receives nearly the same amount of heat from the Sun year round. There are no seasons on the equator. The changes in seasons are bigger the farther north or south you get from the equator. The North and South Poles have only two seasons. The Sun never rises during the middle of winter. The Sun never sets during most of the summer. Much of the United States and southern Canada has four seasons every year.

A meteorologist tracks the weather.

FIND OUT MORE ABOUT...

Weather Forecasting

"What will the weather be like today?" People want to know if it will be warm or cold, if it will be windy, or if it might rain or snow. The answers help them decide what to wear or whether to go outside at all. A **meteorologist** (mee-tee-uh-RAW-luh-jist) is someone who studies the atmosphere and the weather and tries to answer these questions. **Weather forecasting** is the science of predicting what the weather will be like for that day or for the next few days.

Meteorologists measure the air's temperature, pressure, and amount of moisture, or **humidity**. They measure the direction and speed of the wind. They also watch pictures of the Earth's weather taken by satellites in space. These pictures can follow storms and show where they are going. Meteorologists use all of this information to make a **weather report** about what will happen. The report may be for the local area, for the country, or for the whole world. It says what the temperatures might be for that day. The report also says if there might be sunshine, clouds, wind, rain, snow, tornadoes, or hurricanes.

■ Habitats

Life on the Earth depends on a balance between the environment and the organisms that live within it. The areas in which specific plants and animals normally live and grow are called **habitats**. Some habitats are as small as the shade under a rock. Most habitats are larger areas that contain many species of plants and animals. Often, only certain kinds of plants and animals can survive in a specific area. The habitat succeeds through the interaction between animal, plant, and the environment.

A habitat includes all the plants and animals that live in it.

● The Ocean as a Habitat

There are many different habitats within the **ocean**. All the oceans of the world are filled with saltwater. Some parts of the oceans are warmer and colder at different times of the year. A condition called **El Niño** (ell NEEN-yoh) is when a large part of the Pacific Ocean becomes warmer than usual. A condition called **La Niña** (lah NEEN-yah) is when a large part of the Pacific Ocean becomes colder than usual. These changes can affect the weather around the world. Temperature changes can cause some types of fish to die. Mammals and fish that eat other fish may also die or migrate somewhere else to look for food.

There are different areas within the oceans where plants and animals can live. Some live near the shore in **tidepools**. Tides go in and out. There are times when the habitat is exposed to air and times when it is exposed to water. The creatures that live there must be

Sea anemones live in tidepools.

tough to withstand the waves. Crabs have hard shells to protect them. Other creatures attach themselves to rocks.

A wide variety of creatures live in **coral reefs**. Colonies of coral provide homes for many small fish. They swim in and out of the coral to protect themselves from larger fish who might eat them.

Many sea creatures live in the open ocean. Some live close to the surface because they need sunlight. Seaweed needs light for photosynthesis. (To find out about photosynthesis, read the chapter "How Plants Grow" in the volume *Plant Life*.) Seaweed never grows deep where light cannot reach it. Other creatures have adapted to live deep under the sea where there is very little light. Some deepwater creatures have no eyes.

GETTING TO KNOW...

Jacques Cousteau

Jacques Cousteau (koo-STOH) was born in France in 1910. He joined the French navy. Cousteau tested how long he could hold his breath underwater. He wanted to go on long dives. Big diving suits and hoses were used for breathing underwater. They did not work well. Cousteau helped develop the Aqua-Lung (AW-kwuh-lung). It was a device for controlling the flow of gases that could be used with a small tank of air.

Cousteau studied the world under the ocean. He used a ship called the *Calypso* (kuh-LIP-soh) as his laboratory. He explored sunken ships on the ocean floor. He filmed sea animals like sharks, whales, dolphins, and turtles. He went more than one mile or kilometer down into the ocean.

● Lakes and Rivers

L akes and rivers are areas of freshwater. This means that their water is not salty, like in the ocean. Some **lakes** are very large and deep. The Great Lakes in North America are almost like small oceans. Other lakes are small and shallow. Different lakes can have very different temperatures. They can have different mixtures of chemicals. These things depend on the surrounding climate and the source of the water that flows into the lake. Lakes that get water from mountain streams of melted snow can be cold.

Some otters live in rivers.

Rivers can be large or small. The Mississippi River in the United States, the Nile in Egypt, and the Amazon in South America are very large, wide rivers. They flow very quickly and have strong currents. Few plants can grow in fast rivers because the water is always moving. Slower rivers often have many plants growing on their shores.

Lakes and other bodies of water that stay still have much more plant life. Many animals can live in lakes and rivers, such as otters, turtles, hippos, and all kinds of freshwater fish.

● Swamps and Marshes

Swamps and marshes are areas on land where the soil is always covered in water. This happens when the water cannot drain well or when it rains very often. These habitats are very important for the environment. The blanket of plants that grow in them prevent the soil from washing away. The water also makes dead material decay faster and keeps the soil healthy. These habitats are also called wetlands. Some wetlands are huge and cover a lot of land, such as the Everglades in Florida.

Swamps and marshes are very muddy. Swamps have more woody plants, while marshes have more grasses. Some marshes are filled with saltwater. They are often flooded by the ocean. The plants and animals in them must be able to live in different levels of water and salt. Other

Tall trees can grow in swamps.

marshes have freshwater. Reeds often grow in freshwater marshes. Another type of marsh is called a bog. It starts out as a freshwater marsh. Then nutrients in the soil are washed away by moving water. The soil that is left behind contains a lot of acid. Mosses grow well in bogs.

● Deserts

Many people think that **deserts** are dry places where it is always hot and it never rains. A few deserts are like that, but most are not. Deserts often get several inches or centimeters of rain every year. This rain may fall in only one short period. Some deserts have flash floods when too much rain falls at once. Other deserts have areas with more water where trees and other green plants can grow. One of these areas is called an **oasis** (oh-AY-sis). Temperatures in deserts can be very hot during the day and very cold at night. Some deserts have piles of sand blown about by strong winds. These piles are called dunes.

Many different plants can survive in the desert.

Most deserts are much more than sand. Many plants and animals can live in these conditions. Animals like lizards and rabbits dig, or burrow, underground to escape the heat. Other animals only move around at night when it is cooler. Some plants and animals have ways of keeping water in their bodies. Camels can live a long time without food or water by using the fat in the humps on their backs. Plants like the cactus can hold extra water in their stems.

People may ride camels in the deserts of Africa and the Middle East.

● Prairies

Vast grasslands, or **prairies** (PRAIR-reez), are found throughout the world. In Africa, grasslands are called **savanna** (suh-VAH-nuh). In Asia, they are called **steppe** (step). The prairies of North America are low habitats. Very few trees grow there. Most of the plant life is low to the ground. This helps plants survive when there is little water available. Grasses provide food sources for many grazing animals. Huge herds of buffalo once lived on the wild prairies of North America. They ate the grass for food. Because grasses grow from the bottom of their stems, they grow back easily. As the herds moved, they trampled seeds into the ground. Their droppings provided nutrients and fertilizer that encouraged new growth.

A buffalo grazing on a prairie.

Farmers may grow wheat on prairies.

Many animals live underground in the prairies. Prairie dogs live in packs and dig burrows underground for shelter and protection. Mice and other rodents also dig tunnels underground. Mice eat the seeds and grass that are all around. Animals like coyotes often eat mice.

Some areas of the prairies are used for farming. Giant fields of wheat and corn can stretch out for miles. Grains harvested from these fields are used by humans for food.

● Forests

There are different kinds of **forests** throughout the world. Some forests have many trees tightly packed together. Monkeys and squirrels can live in these trees away from predators. Other forests have trees that are spread out. The pine forests in the Pacific Northwest have many trees that need a lot of space to grow. They provide homes for birds of prey like owls. It is easier for birds to hunt animals that live on the ground in these forests.

Forests provide homes for birds of prey like owls.

Redwoods grow in a forest in the Pacific Northwest.

Forests also provide animals with shelter from bad weather. A single tree in a forest can provide a habitat for a variety of other living things. Birds may nest in a tree for protection. Insects might also find a home in the tree. Some birds eat insects. The tree itself can provide food through its fruits and seeds. A tree that falls down can provide a home to many animals on the ground.

Forest habitats are frequently destroyed by humans. Some forests are cleared to make room for farming or construction. Other forests are damaged by chemical waste and pollution. Sometimes new forests are planted where old ones had been chopped down. This is called **reforestation**.

FIND OUT MORE ABOUT...

Tropical Rainforests

The tropical areas of the Earth are found around the equator. They usually have dense forests that get a lot of rain. These rainforests are very important to the planet. Nowhere else in the world can such a variety of plant and animal life be found. Over half of all the species of plants and animals on Earth live in tropical rainforests. The Amazon Rainforest in South America is one of the largest forests in the world. Rainforests also turn a lot of the carbon dioxide in the air into oxygen through photosynthesis. They are like giant air filters for the planet.

Trees in the rainforest grow tall. They must fight each other for sunlight. The tops of the trees make up the **canopy**. Most of the animals in the rainforests live in the canopy. There, they find sunlight and a lot of food. The temperature is cooler and it is not as sunny underneath the canopy. Animals live there, but not as many different kinds as in the canopy. Sloths move very slowly and eat fruit and insects that live on the trees. Snakes like the warm climate of rainforest. Birds of all different shapes and colors fly above the canopy.

● Mountains

The Earth rises high up above the crust where there are mountains. The environment changes as the ground gets higher. The different habitats on a mountain as it rises are called zones. Along the base of most mountains are forests. The forests will only grow up a mountain to a certain point. The tree line is the height above which trees will not grow. Other plants will grow beyond the tree line. These plants tend to be small plants that can withstand cold temperatures and high winds.

Animals who live above the tree line tend to be ready for cold weather. Mammals like deer and mountain goats have big hearts and lungs. These help them breathe in the high altitude and cold. Many insects survive well in this habitat. Ants and other insects without wings can stay low to the ground to avoid the wind.

Higher up a mountain it gets really cold. The point up a mountain where snow stays year around is called the **snow line**. The closer to the equator a mountain is the higher the snow line will be. Mountains in the arctic or polar areas of the world are

Mountain goats can live at high altitudes.

often entirely above the snow line. Very few plants and animals live in this cold region.

DID YOU KNOW...

There Is Life at the South Pole

Antarctica is the coldest place on Earth! Many different life forms live in this polar habitat. On the coast of Antarctica there are flightless birds called penguins. They can swim under the ice to eat fish and plankton. They lay eggs on the land.

■ The Environment in Danger

Everything on the Earth is connected in some way. Changes on the land can affect the air. Changes in the air can affect the water. Damage to one thing always affects something else. It is easy to damage the Earth. The human population of our planet is growing very fast. The environment suffers as more people need the Earth's resources. Human activity can hurt the land, air, and sea. People have caused the destruction of many habitats. Many species of plants and animals are endangered or extinct. The machines that humans use make pollution that can cause problems in the environment.

● Fires

Fires can burn homes and other buildings. They can burn nature too. Forest fires and brush fires destroy trees and other plants. Fires can start in many ways. People sometimes start fires on purpose. This is called **arson**. Other fires are started by accident. People who are camping may not put out their campfires. People who smoke may throw away cigarettes that are still burning. Oil and rubber tires give off dangerous gases when they burn. Humans do the most harm when they burn too much land. Some people set fires in rainforests to clear the land for farming. Many people in Asia became sick because so many fires were set on the islands of Indonesia (in-duh-NEE-zhuh).

Fires can also start naturally when lightning strikes the ground. People can actually hurt the environment by putting out natural fires. Fire clears away dead plants so that new ones can grow. Some seeds will sprout only after they have burned.

● Smog

Smog is fog mixed with smoke and other chemicals. It makes the air look brown or dirty. Smog has chemicals that hurt the lungs. It is especially dangerous to people who have trouble breathing. Smog can develop in two ways. One type of smog forms when people burn fuel that has a chemical called sulfur. Coal has a lot of sulfur. This smog is common in the eastern United States and Europe. Another type of smog forms from chemicals in automobile exhaust. These fumes come out of cars when they use gasoline. Sunlight changes these chemicals. This is called **photochemical** (foh-toh-KEH-mih-kul) **smog**. Places with a lot of cars, like cities, have this type of smog. Special gasoline and laws about how cars burn fuel can help.

Smog makes the air brown and hazy.

● Acid Rain

Acid rain is more acid than natural rain. (To find out more about acids, read the volume *Chemistry*.) Acid rain develops when forms of sulfur and nitrogen called **oxides** (AWK-sides) mix with water in the atmosphere. The acids that are created fall back down to Earth when it rains. The pollution comes from factories in the Midwest, but winds blow the chemicals north and east. Some acid rain comes from natural sources like dead plants. Most of it comes from human sources like cars and factories.

Oxides can travel a long way before they come back down as acid rain. Acid rain can damage lakes, forests, and soil. Fish die when the water in lakes has too much acid. Acid rain can also hurt buildings. Statues made of stone can be eaten away by acid rain. The areas with the worst damage have been the eastern United States and the southeastern part of Canada.

This statue has been eroded by acid rain.

● **Deforestation**

Trees are important to the environment. They feed many animals and give them homes. They keep the air and soil healthy. Trees also provide people with important things like fuel, paper, wood, and food. The environment is in danger when people cut down too many trees without planting enough new ones. A forest may die or be cut down completely. This is called **deforestation** (dee-for-uh-STAY-shun). Tropical rainforests are the most endangered forests in the world.

GETTING TO KNOW...

F. Sherwood Rowland and Mario Molina

F. Sherwood Rowland was born in Ohio in 1927. In 1964, he became the head of the new chemistry department at the University of California at Irvine. Rowland began to study **chlorofluorocarbons** (klor-oh-flor-oh-KAR-bunz), or CFCs. These chemicals were being used in spray cans, refrigerators, and air conditioners. He wondered what happened to CFCs in the atmosphere.

Mario Molina was born in Mexico in 1943. He joined Rowland's research team in Irvine in 1973. Together, they discovered that CFCs break apart and form atoms of chlorine (KLOR-een). Chlorine destroys the ozone that protects life on Earth from radiation. Rowland and Molina helped to create the worldwide ban on CFCs. They won the Nobel Prize for their research.

FIND OUT MORE ABOUT...

The Greenhouse Effect

Humans and other animals exhale carbon dioxide when they breathe. Normally, plants filter this gas out of the air during photosynthesis. Burning oil, coal, and wood makes extra carbon dioxide and other gases. They are called **greenhouse gases**. These gases form a layer around the Earth. This layer allows sunlight to pass through to the surface. But it prevents heat from escaping into outer space. Over time, the Earth gets hotter and hotter. This is called the **greenhouse effect** or **global warming**.

Global warming will threaten all life on the planet if it continues. Ice at the North Pole and the South Pole will melt as the temperature of the Earth increases. This will cause the water level of the ocean to rise. Much of the Earth will become flooded. Eventually, it will become so hot that all life on the planet will die.

People are taking steps to reduce the threat of global warming. Fuels that burn cleaner are being used. They do not produce as many greenhouse gases. Factories are finding ways of manufacturing that cause less harm to the environment. Governments are setting goals for reducing greenhouse gas emissions. It is possible for people to prevent global warming.

■ People Who Study the Earth

Throughout history, people have always wanted to understand the planet we live on. They wanted to know why the weather changes from hot to cold and back again. They wanted to know why it rains or snows and what lightning and thunder are. They wanted to know why volcanoes erupt and why earthquakes move the ground. Some people created stories about gods and heroes to explain these things. Other people looked to religion for answers. Other people, called scientists, studied nature. Earth science is the study of the Earth and all the forces that can affect it.

A geologist examines stones.

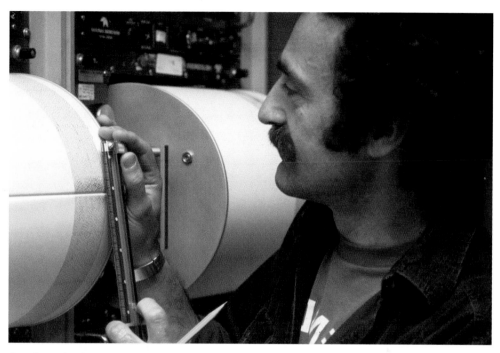

A seismologist uses a seismograph to study earthquakes.

There are different fields within earth science. **Geologists** (jee-AW-luh-jists) study the history of the Earth by looking at rocks. **Paleontologists** (pay-lee-on-TAW-luh-jists) dig up fossils to learn what the world was like in the past. **Seismologists** (size-MAW-luh-jists) measure earthquakes and study the movement of the continental plates. They sometimes try to predict when future earthquakes will occur. **Volcanologists** (vall-kuh-NAW-lu-jists) study volcanoes and their effect on the environment. Meteorologists study the atmosphere. They watch the weather and try to predict when and where storms, tornadoes, or hurricanes will happen. **Oceanographers** (oh-shuh-NAW-gruh-furz) study the ocean. They measure how deep the ocean is, the plants and animals that live within it, and how people use it as a resource. **Ecologists** (ih-KOL-uh-jists) try to understand how living things and their environments affect each other. **Environmentalists** (in-vi-run-MEN-tul-ustz) try to protect the environment from pollution and other dangers.

Learning about these things helps people use the resources of the Earth wisely. Human beings must understand that everything they do affects the planet that all living things share.

Index